The Art of the Game: Volleyball Mindset

SPIKE PARENTS

Copyright © 2024 Spike Parents
All rights reserved.
ISBN: 9798336587388

DEDICATION

To all the athletes who dare to dream big and pursue excellence with relentless passion. Keep striving, keep believing, and never forget that the journey itself is as important as the destination. You are the true embodiment of dedication, and your pursuit of greatness inspires us all.

THE ART OF THE GAME: VOLLEYBALL MINDSET

CONTENTS

ACKNOWLEDGMENTS

To the readers - thank you for your curiosity, your passion for growth, and your commitment to becoming the best version of yourselves. Whether you are just beginning your journey or are well along the path, it is your desire to learn and improve that gives this book its purpose. I hope these words resonate with you and serve as a guide as you continue to chase your dreams.

To the coaches, mentors, and teammates who shape and support athletes every day - your influence is immeasurable. You are the pillars of strength and knowledge that help athletes grow, not only in their sport but in life. Your wisdom and guidance echo through these pages, as do the countless hours you spend molding champions both on and off the field.

Lastly, to every athlete who opens this book and finds even a small spark of inspiration within its chapters - thank you for allowing me to be a part of your journey. Remember that the pursuit of greatness is a lifelong adventure, filled with ups and downs, victories and lessons. embrace every moment and know that your dedication and hard work will always pave the way for your success.

THE ART OF THE GAME: VOLLEYBALL MINDSET

INTRODUCTION

"Success is not final, failure is not fatal: it is the courage to continue that counts."
— Winston Churchill

This book focuses on developing a champion's mindset for young female volleyball players, guiding them through mental preparation, training, discipline, resilience, and the journey to excellence. It emphasizes the importance of self-awareness, dealing with internal fears, and using visualization and goal setting as tools for success.

The chapters cover key themes such as treating the court as a battlefield for self-discovery, the role of discipline and routine in shaping character, the value of teamwork, and turning failures into learning experiences. It also explores handling pressure, pushing beyond limits, and maintaining a healthy competitive spirit.

However, this guide is **not** for everyone.

"The Art of the Game" is not for those with a negative or narrow mindset - those who believe that their abilities are fixed, and that success is reserved for the lucky or the naturally gifted. It is not for those who are unwilling to put in the hard work, who are content with complacency, or who shy away from the discomfort that comes with growth. If you are looking for quick fixes or shortcuts, this book will not provide them.

This guide is for the athletes who understand that the path to greatness is paved with discipline, perseverance, and an unyielding commitment to self-improvement. It is for those who are willing to embrace challenges, learn from failures, and continually push their limits. If you are ready to cultivate a mindset that not only improves your game but also enhances every aspect of your life, then this book is for you.

Prepare to embark on a journey that will challenge you, inspire you, and ultimately transform the way you approach both your sport and your life. **"The Art of the Game"** is your companion on the road to excellence - are you ready to take the first step?

Before reading the book, below are **8 practical steps** that you can start doing today for continuous improvement in your athletic journey:

1. Perform a Self-Assessment

- **Set Aside Time:** Dedicate time at the end of each week or after important games to reflect on your performance.
- **Write It Down:** Create a journal where you document your thoughts. Break down your performance into strengths and areas for improvement. Be honest with yourself—acknowledge what you did well and where you struggled.
- **Identify Patterns:** Look for recurring patterns in your performance. Are there certain situations where you consistently excel or struggle? Understanding these can help you focus on specific areas that need attention.

2. Reflect on Successes and Failures

- **Analyze Successes**: Think back to moments when you performed exceptionally well. What was your mindset? What preparation did you do that contributed to your success? Document these factors so you can replicate them in the future.
- **Learn from Failures:** Don't shy away from examining your mistakes. Consider what went wrong—were you distracted, overconfident, or technically off? Understanding the root causes of your failures helps you avoid them in the future.

3. Seek External Feedback

- **Talk to Your Coach:** Schedule regular check-ins with your coach to discuss your performance. Ask for specific feedback on your strengths and areas where you need to improve and learn to listen his/her point of view.
- **Engage with Teammates:** Get feedback from your teammates. They may notice things you do not, such as your communication on the court or your body language during high-pressure situations.

4. Set Goals Based on Your Self-Assessment

- **Specific Goals:** Based on your self-assessment, set clear, specific goals. For example, if you've identified that your serve accuracy needs improvement, set a goal to increase your serving percentage by a certain amount over the next month.

- **Create an Action Plan:** Break your goals down into actionable steps. This could involve additional drills, specific exercises, or mental training techniques.

5. Monitor Your Progress

- **Keep a Progress Journal:** Regularly update your journal with notes on how you're progressing towards your goals. Celebrate small victories to keep yourself motivated.
- **Adjust as Needed:** If you are not seeing the progress you hoped for, reassess your action plan and make adjustments. Continuous improvement is about being flexible and adapting to what works best for you.

6. Embrace a Growth Mindset

- **Stay Positive:** View challenges as opportunities to grow rather than setbacks. Understand that improvement takes time and effort and be patient with yourself.
- **Focus on the Journey:** Remember that self-awareness and improvement are ongoing processes. The goal is not just to fix weaknesses but to continually evolve as an athlete.

7. Apply What You Learn

- **In Practice:** Use your insights during training to focus on areas you've identified as needing improvement. For example, if you struggle under pressure, simulate high-pressure situations during practice.
- **During Games:** Apply the lessons you've learned from your self-assessment in real-game scenarios. Stay mindful of your strengths and be conscious of how you handle your weaknesses.

8. Continuously Reassess

- **Ongoing Process:** Make self-awareness a regular part of your routine. Regularly revisit your self-assessments, set new goals, and continue seeking feedback.
- **Long-Term Growth:** Understand that this process will serve you not just in the current season but throughout your entire athletic career and beyond. It's a tool for lifelong improvement and success.

By consistently applying these steps, you'll build a deeper understanding of yourself as an athlete, allowing you to make targeted improvements and achieve greater success in your sport. Let's begin!

CHAPTER 1: KNOW YOURSELF

"A lot of people told me I would never be
a good volleyball player or high jumper because
I never specialized. But I always knew that I could,
believed I could, so I didn't listen to what they said.
I just followed my heart and did it."
– Tayyiba Haneef
(former American volleyball player who
won silver medals at both the 2008 Beijing
and the 2012 London Olympics)

The importance of self-awareness and self-criticism

Imagine that you are a young volleyball player, known for her powerful spikes and quick reflexes. You have playing for your high school team for several years and have always been one of the top performers.

However, this season has been different. Despite putting in the same amount of effort, you feel like you are stuck in a rut. Your spikes lack their usual power, your serves are inconsistent, and you are making uncharacteristic errors during crucial moments of the game.

As the season progresses, you start to doubt your abilities and feel the pressure mounting. You are frustrated, as you know you have the potential to do better, but something is holding you back.

You need to pause and take a step back from the immediate pressures of competition. It's time for you to engage in self-awareness, a critical tool for any athlete facing a slump or struggling to reach their full potential. Self-awareness involves a deep, honest look at oneself to identify both strengths and weaknesses. This process allows an athlete to understand what is working and what needs to be improved.

What Should You Do?

Reflection on strengths and areas for improvement

You can reflect on strengths and areas for improvement by doing the following:

1. **Perform a Written Self-Assessment:** You should begin by writing down your thoughts, breaking down your recent performances. You can start by listing your strengths, the skills you believe are solid, and that you can rely on during a game. For example, you might note that your quick reflexes on defense and your ability to read the opponent's plays are strengths you are consistently proud of.

   Next, you should honestly assess your weaknesses. You might recognize that your spike accuracy has been off, or that your mental focus wanes during high-pressure moments. This part of the assessment is crucial, as it requires you to confront the areas where you feel vulnerable. Writing this down helps in organizing thoughts and provides a clear picture of where you stand.

2. **Reflect on Moments of Success and Failure:** You should take time to reflect on both your successful and unsuccessful

moments. You might recall a game earlier in the season where you executed a perfect spike that turned the momentum in your team's favor. What was your mindset at that moment? What preparation did you do that contributed to that success?

Conversely, you should analyze a time when you missed an easy serve or faltered under pressure. What was different? Were you mentally distracted? Was your technique off? Understanding these moments can reveal patterns and help you recognize what factors contribute to your performance, both positively and negatively.

3. **Seek Feedback from Teammates and Coaches:** Sometimes, an external perspective is necessary to gain a full understanding of one's abilities. You should seek feedback from your coach and teammates, asking them for an honest evaluation of your performance. A coach might notice that your footwork has become sluggish, which could be affecting your spike accuracy. A teammate might point out that you seem more hesitant than usual, suggesting that confidence might be an underlying issue.

By gathering these insights, you will have a clear understanding of who you are as an athlete, which will allow you to work on your weaknesses and maximize your strengths, leading to more consistent and effective performance.

Consider **Michael Jordan**, one of the greatest basketball players of all time. Even at the peak of his career, Jordan continuously practiced self-awareness. After every game, he would review tapes, not just to celebrate his successes but to scrutinize his mistakes. He would look for patterns in his performance—moments where he hesitated or made the wrong decision. Jordan would then work relentlessly on those weaknesses, turning them into strengths. His ability to honestly assess his game and seek feedback from coaches and teammates played a significant role in his evolution as an athlete, allowing him to perform consistently at the highest level.

By practicing self-awareness, you will develop a clear understanding of who you are as an athlete. This process will allow you to confront your weaknesses without fear, transforming them into areas of growth. Simultaneously, you will gain confidence in your strengths, understanding how to leverage them effectively during games.

With this newfound clarity, you can approach training with a targeted mindset, focusing on specific areas that need improvement while reinforcing what you already do well. Over time, this will lead to more consistent and effective performance on the court. You will not only regain your form but surpass your previous levels, armed with the knowledge that you have the power to continually evolve as an athlete.

This process of self-awareness and continuous improvement is not just a tool for overcoming a challenging season; it's a lifelong approach that will serve you throughout your athletic career and beyond.

Main takeaway from this Chapter:

- You should practice self-awareness by taking a step back from the pressures of competition to engage in an honest self-assessment. This involves reflecting on your strengths, identifying areas for improvement, and seeking feedback from your coach and teammates.
- By writing down your thoughts and analyzing both her successes and failures, you can gain a comprehensive understanding of her performance. This process will allow you to address weaknesses without fear and leverage your strengths more effectively.
- Over time, this targeted approach will lead to more consistent and improved performance, helping you not only overcome your current challenges but also continue evolving throughout your athletic career.

We believe that here we are discussing naturally talented athletes but, in this guide, we will address that talent alone is not enough. Effort and dedication surpass talent—when we take a realistic analysis, of course. And a minimum level of aptitude is necessary.

CHAPTER 2: THE INNER ENEMY

"The Olympics is such a draining process for the athletes when it's multiple days of competition, so you definitely have to be on top of your mental, as well as your physical. So as long as we're doing that, then, we're good."
- Simone Biles
(Gymnastic athlete)

Dealing with Fear, Doubt, and Insecurity

Imagine that you, a standout volleyball player on your team, have been preparing all season for the upcoming championship match. Your team has made it to the finals, and the weight of the entire season's work seems to rest on this one game.

As you lie in bed the night before the match, fear and doubt begin to creep in. You start questioning yourself: "What if I miss the crucial serve? What if I let my team down? Am I good enough to handle the pressure?"

These thoughts swirl in your mind, making you feel anxious and uncertain. The fear of failure looms large, and you struggle to shake it off, feeling overwhelmed by the magnitude of the upcoming challenge.

You must confront your fears and doubts head-on instead of trying to push them away. It's natural to feel afraid before a big moment, but the key is to acknowledge these feelings and use them as motivation rather than letting them paralyze you.

By recognizing that fear is a normal part of competition, you can start to take control of your mindset, transforming that fear into determination and focus.

What Should You Do?

Strategies to Win Mental Battles

1. **Use Visualization Techniques:** we will talk more about this in the next Chapter. Visualization includes closing your eyes and mentally walking through the upcoming match, imagining yourself in different scenarios where you might feel pressure. You should visualize yourself stepping onto the court with confidence, feeling the energy of the crowd, and executing each play with precision. For example, you can picture yourself serving the ball perfectly, your body moving fluidly as you make decisive plays, and the satisfaction of seeing the ball hit the floor on the opponent's side.

   In this visualization, you should focus on the details: the sound of the ball hitting the court, the sight of your teammates celebrating, and the calmness in your breath as you prepare for each serve. By repeatedly visualizing these successful outcomes, you can train your brain to anticipate success rather than failure, making these mental images a reality when you step onto the court.

2. **Practice Positive Affirmations:** You should incorporate positive affirmations into your daily routine, especially leading up to the big match. These are short, powerful statements that reinforce your confidence and capabilities. Examples might include:

"I am prepared for this moment."

"I trust in my skills and my training."

"I am strong, focused, and ready to perform."

You should repeat these affirmations every morning and night, and even silently to yourself during the game. Over time, these affirmations will help override the negative thoughts and reinforce a positive, confident mindset.

3. **Confront Small Challenges Voluntarily Off the Court:** To build mental toughness, you should actively seek out small challenges in your daily life that push you out of your comfort zone. This could be as simple as trying a new workout that you find intimidating, that one more rep, one more mile, or taking on a leadership role in a group project at school. These experiences help you develop the resilience needed to face larger challenges, like a high-stakes volleyball match.

By consistently putting yourself in situations that cause discomfort, you will train your mind to stay calm and composed under pressure. You will learn to manage the anxiety that comes with stepping into the unknown, and this mental training will translate directly to your performance on the court.

By following these steps, you will become mentally stronger and more resilient. The fear and doubt that once seemed overwhelming will now serve as fuel for your determination. You will approach the championship match with a clear, focused mind, ready to turn pressure into a catalyst for success.

When you step onto the court, you will have already won the internal battle against your fears. This victory will give you the confidence to play at your best, knowing that you have the mental strength to handle whatever comes your way. As a result, you will perform with greater consistency and effectiveness, turning potential obstacles into opportunities to showcase your abilities.

In the end, you will not only excel in the big match but will also carry these mental tools forward, using them to overcome challenges in future competitions and in life. By conquering the inner enemy, you will unlock your full potential as an athlete, confident and ready to face any challenge that comes your way.

Michael Phelps and the 2008 Beijing Olympics

Before the 2008 Olympics, **Michael Phelps** was already a world-renowned swimmer, but the expectations placed on him were astronomical. He was aiming to break the record for the most gold medals won in a single Olympics, a feat that required perfection in every race. The weight of this goal created intense pressure, leading to moments of fear and doubt. Phelps began to question whether he could live up to the expectations and achieve what many believed was impossible. The fear of failure, of not meeting these expectations, became his greatest inner enemy.

What Michael Phelps Did?

1. Visualization Techniques

Phelps was known for his rigorous mental preparation, which included detailed visualization. Every night before a race, Phelps would lie down and mentally rehearse the perfect race in his mind. He visualized every stroke, every turn, and every possible scenario, including things going wrong—such as his goggles filling with water or a bad start. This mental imagery was so vivid that when something did go wrong during an actual race (like in the 200-meter butterfly final in Beijing, where his goggles filled with water), he remained calm and executed the race almost flawlessly, relying on his muscle memory and mental rehearsal.

2. Positive Affirmations

Phelps also used positive affirmations and self-talk to build his confidence. His coach, Bob Bowman, would often reinforce Phelps' belief in his preparation and abilities. Phelps constantly reminded himself that he had done everything possible to prepare, and that he was ready for the challenge. This helped him override the negative thoughts and doubts that naturally arose under such immense pressure.

3. Confronting Small Challenges

In training, Bowman would create situations designed to make Phelps uncomfortable, such as purposefully breaking his rhythm during practice or asking him to swim without a particular piece of equipment. These small, controlled challenges helped Phelps develop a mindset of resilience and adaptability. By repeatedly facing and overcoming minor obstacles, Phelps trained his mind to stay focused and composed, even when things didn't go as planned.

4. What was the result?

Phelps' mental preparation paid off spectacularly. At the 2008 Beijing Olympics, he won eight gold medals, breaking the record for the most gold medals won in a single Olympic Games. His ability to conquer his inner enemy - fear and doubt - allowed him to perform under extraordinary pressure and achieve what many thought was impossible.

Phelps' story is a powerful example of how an athlete can use visualization, positive affirmations, and confronting small challenges to conquer fear and self-doubt. By doing so, Phelps not only achieved greatness in his sport but also set a new standard for mental toughness in athletics.

"You play as you train."

This quote emphasizes the direct relationship between how you practice and how you perform in actual competition. The idea is that the habits, intensity, focus, and discipline you bring to your training sessions will directly influence how you play in a real game or match.

If you train with high intensity, precision, and a strong work ethic, those qualities will likely carry over into your performance during competition. Conversely, if you approach training with a lack of focus or effort, your performance in the game will reflect that. Essentially, this quote highlights that there are no shortcuts to success; the way you prepare is the way you will perform when it counts.

This mindset encourages athletes to treat every practice as if it were a real game, ensuring that they develop the skills, mental toughness, and consistency needed to excel under pressure.

Main takeaway from this Chapter:

- You need to confront your fears and doubts head-on, recognizing them as natural parts of competition and using them to fuel her determination rather than allowing them to paralyze her.
- You can do this by visualizing successful outcomes in high-pressure situations, practicing positive affirmations to reinforce her confidence, and voluntarily facing small challenges off the court to build mental toughness.

- By consistently applying these strategies, you will transform your fear into focus and approach your matches with a clear, determined mindset. This mental strength will not only help you excel in the immediate challenge but also equip you to handle future pressures, allowing you to consistently perform at your best and unlock your full potential as an athlete.
- There are no shortcuts to success; the way you prepare is the way you will perform when it counts.

CHAPTER 3: VISUALIZE VICTORY

"Adversity, if you allow it to,
will fortify you and
make you the best you can be."
- Kerri Walsh Jennings
(former Beach American volleyball player who
won gold medals at 2004 Athens, 2008 Beijing
and the 2012 London Olympics
with her partner Misty May-Treanor)

The Power of Visualization and Goal Setting

A well-known example of an elite athlete who extensively used visualization is **Muhammad Ali**, one of the greatest boxers of all time. Ali was famous for his mental preparation, which included vivid visualization. He would mentally rehearse his fights, imagining himself winning each round, outmaneuvering his opponents, and delivering knockout punches.

Ali's visualization wasn't just about winning; he would envision the entire process—the way he would move, how he would counter his opponent's moves, and the exact punches he would throw.

Ali's mental rehearsal was so detailed that he would often predict the round in which he would knock out his opponent, and more often than not, he was right. This intense mental preparation allowed Ali to enter the ring with unshakable confidence, knowing that he had already "won" the fight many times over in his mind. His visualization techniques were a key factor in his dominance in the ring and contributed significantly to his legendary career.

What Should You Do?

Embrace Visualization as a Tool for Success

You need to incorporate the powerful tool of visualization into her preparation. Visualization is a mental rehearsal technique where the athlete vividly imagines themselves performing successfully in their sport. By visualizing positive outcomes and perfect execution, you can prepare your mind to replicate that success in real-life scenarios. Visualization is not just about seeing the outcome; it's about feeling the emotions, engaging the senses, and mentally experiencing every detail of the performance.

1. **Create a Clear Mental Picture:**

You should find a quiet place where you will not be interrupted; close your eyes and create a detailed mental image of yourself on the volleyball court. You should visualize every aspect of the game, starting from the moment you step onto the court. You should imagine the feel of the ball in your hands, the texture of the court under your shoes, the sound of your teammates' voices, and the roar of the crowd.

In this mental rehearsal, you should visualize yourself executing each play with precision and confidence. You should see yourself serving the ball with perfect form, the ball spinning exactly as you intend, landing in the opponent's court just out of their reach. You should imagine the power and timing of your spikes, the ball smashing down into the court as your opponents scramble to react. The key is to make these images as vivid and realistic as possible, engaging all your senses.

2. **Focus on Process, Not Just Outcome**

While it is important for you to visualize the successful outcome of her actions, you should also focus on the process that leads to those outcomes. This means visualizing your preparation before the serve, your approach to the net before a spike, and the way you communicate with your teammates during a play. By mentally rehearsing these processes, you will be better prepared to execute them during an actual game, as they will feel familiar and second nature.

3. **Incorporate Emotions and Confidence**

Visualization is not just about seeing the play unfold; it is also about feeling the emotions associated with success. You should imagine the confidence you feel as you step up to serve, the satisfaction of executing a perfect spike, and the exhilaration of celebrating a point with your team. These positive emotions help to reinforce your belief in your abilities, making it easier to access that confidence during real matches.

You should repeat this visualization exercise regularly, ideally every day, especially before practices and games. The more you practice visualization, the stronger the mental pathways become, making it easier for your mind and body to replicate the successful performances you have been rehearsing.

4. **Combine Visualization with Physical Practice**

After each visualization session, you should immediately translate those mental images into physical practice. For instance, after visualizing a perfect serve, you should head to the court and practice your serves, focusing on replicating the exact motions you visualized. This combination of mental and physical practice helps to solidify the connection between your mind and body, making it more likely that you will perform at your best during actual games.

What Will Be the Result?

By consistently using visualization techniques, you will notice a shift in your performance. The gap between your effort and your results will start to close as your mind becomes better aligned with your physical capabilities. Visualization will help you to build confidence, reduce anxiety, and improve your focus during games.

As you continue to visualize success, you will find that your movements on the court become more fluid and natural, as if you have already done them a hundred times before—because, in your mind, you have. The plays that once felt difficult or inconsistent will become second nature, and your performance will start to reflect the hard work you have put in.

In time, you will not only perform at the level you know you are capable of, but you may also exceed your own expectations. Visualization will have prepared your mind to lead your body to victory, transforming you into the player you always knew you could be. This newfound mental strength will be a cornerstone of your success, both in volleyball and in any future challenges you face.

Dedicate 10 Minutes Daily to Visualization

To start, find a quiet space where you won't be interrupted. Sit or lie down comfortably, close your eyes, and take a few deep breaths to center yourself. For the next 10 minutes, immerse yourself in the visualization of game situations where you execute every move with precision and confidence.

1. Visualize Each Move Perfectly

Begin by imagining yourself in specific game scenarios that are critical to your performance. For example, if you're a volleyball player, you might start by visualizing yourself serving the ball. Picture the exact technique: the way you grip the ball, the position of your feet, the smooth motion of your arm as you swing, and the ball's trajectory as it flies over the net and lands exactly where you intended. Focus on the feeling of the serve - the strength in your muscles, the balance in your stance, and the control you have over the ball.

Next, visualize yourself in other key moments, such as setting up a spike, blocking an opponent's shot, or diving for a difficult save. In each scenario, see yourself executing the move flawlessly, with perfect timing, technique, and outcome. Engage all your senses - hear the sound of the ball, feel the texture of the court, and even smell the air in the gym. The more vivid and detailed your visualization, the more effective it will be.

2. Create a "Mental Movie" of Your Best Possible Performance

Now, extend your visualization into a “mental movie” where you perform at your absolute best throughout an entire game or practice. Imagine the sequence of events from start to finish, watching yourself dominate each aspect of the game. See yourself making perfect serves, communicating effectively with your teammates, and responding instantly to the opponent’s plays.

Replay this mental movie repeatedly in your mind, refining the details each time. Each viewing should be an opportunity to reinforce positive outcomes and to strengthen the neural pathways that connect your mental rehearsal to your physical performance. Over time, this repeated visualization helps to program your brain for success, making it easier for your body to follow suit when it’s time to perform.

3. Visualize Not Only the Game but Also the Process

It is important to visualize not just the game itself, but also the entire process that leads to your peak performance. Start by imagining your pre-game routine. See yourself warming up, stretching, and preparing mentally. Visualize the way you interact with your teammates, the pep talk from your coach, and the energy you bring to the court.

Consider the strategies you will employ during the game. Visualize yourself staying focused, adapting to the opponents' tactics, and making smart decisions under pressure. By visualizing these processes, you prepare your mind to handle every aspect of the game, from the physical to the mental, ensuring that nothing catches you off guard.

What Will Be the Result?

Consistent practice of visualization will have a profound impact on your performance. By repeatedly visualizing perfect execution, you train your brain to expect and achieve that level of performance. Your movements on the court will become more precise, as your body begins to follow the patterns you've rehearsed mentally. Your confidence will also grow, as you've already "lived" the successful moments in your mind, reducing anxiety and increasing your readiness for the real game.

Moreover, visualization helps in decision-making during games. Because you've already envisioned different scenarios and strategies, you'll find yourself reacting faster and more effectively under pressure. Your mind will be programmed to stay calm and focused, allowing you to execute plays with confidence and clarity, even in the most challenging situations.

Examples from Elite Athletes

1. Lindsey Vonn - Skiing

Lindsey Vonn, one of the most successful female ski racers of all time, used visualization as a critical part of her pre-race preparation. Before every race, Vonn would mentally ski the entire course multiple times, visualizing each turn, jump, and section of the slope. This practice helped her memorize the course and anticipate the challenges she would face, allowing her to react quickly and confidently during the actual race. Vonn credits visualization as a key factor in her ability to perform consistently at the highest level.

2. LeBron James - Basketball

LeBron James, one of the greatest basketball players in history, is known for his use of visualization and meditation techniques. Before games, LeBron often visualizes different scenarios he might face on the court, from making a crucial shot to defending against an opponent's play. By visualizing success in these moments, LeBron mentally prepares himself to perform at his best when it matters most. This practice has contributed to his ability to stay calm under pressure and make clutch plays throughout his career.

3. Tiger Woods - Golf

Tiger Woods, widely regarded as one of the greatest golfers of all time, has been using visualization since he was a child. Before every shot, Woods would mentally visualize the entire trajectory of the ball, from the moment of impact to where it would land on the green. This meticulous mental preparation allowed him to focus intensely on each shot and execute it with precision. Woods has often spoken about the importance of visualization in his routine, especially during high-stress moments in major tournaments.

4. Serena Williams - Tennis

Serena Williams, one of the most dominant tennis players ever, uses visualization as part of her mental preparation before matches. Williams often visualizes herself playing specific points, winning key rallies, and lifting trophies. She mentally rehearses her strategies and imagines herself overcoming challenging situations on the court. This visualization helps Serena to approach matches with confidence and determination, contributing to her incredible success in tennis, including multiple Grand Slam titles.

These examples from various sports demonstrate the power of visualization in helping athletes prepare mentally for competition. Visualization makes them look confident, and certain of what they are about to do as they get on the blocks, court, or field.

Andrew Snow explained that this is called the ***flow*** in the book "Run Elite: Train and Think Like the Greatest Runners of All Time". The ***flow*** is the optimal state of consciousness where we feel and perform our best, where focus is so intense that all aspects of performance, both mental and physical, go through the roof. It is about a mental state that believes that what we are doing is important.

Mindset and Confidence

Mindset plays a crucial role in shaping an athlete's confidence, as it directly influences how they perceive challenges, setbacks, and their own abilities. Here's how mindset impacts confidence:

1. Growth Mindset vs. Fixed Mindset

- **Growth Mindset:** An athlete with a growth mindset believes that abilities and intelligence can be developed through effort, learning, and perseverance. This belief fosters confidence because it allows the athlete to view challenges as opportunities for growth rather than threats. When an athlete with a growth mindset encounters a difficult situation, they are more likely to approach it with determination, knowing that their efforts can lead to improvement.
- **Fixed Mindset:** Conversely, an athlete with a fixed mindset believes that their abilities are static and cannot be changed. This mindset can undermine confidence because the athlete may see setbacks as evidence of their limitations. When faced with a challenge, they might avoid it or give up easily, believing that failure is a reflection of their inherent abilities rather than a temporary setback that can be overcome.

2. Self-Belief and Resilience

- **Mindset Shapes Self-Belief:** Confidence is rooted in self-belief - the conviction that one is capable of achieving their goals. A positive mindset reinforces this belief by encouraging athletes to trust in their abilities and the process of improvement. Athletes who believe that they can learn, adapt, and grow are more likely to have the confidence to take risks, try new techniques, and push their limits.
- **Resilience in the Face of Adversity:** A resilient mindset contributes to confidence by helping athletes bounce back from setbacks. When an athlete views challenges as temporary and believes they have the power to overcome them, they maintain confidence even in difficult times. This resilience is crucial for sustaining long-term confidence, as it ensures that the athlete's self-belief remains intact despite occasional failures.

3. Positive vs. Negative Self-Talk

- **Positive Self-Talk:** An athlete's internal dialogue, or self-talk, is heavily influenced by their mindset. A positive, growth-oriented mindset leads to constructive self-talk, where the athlete encourages themselves, focuses on solutions, and stays motivated. This positive reinforcement builds confidence by creating a mental environment where the athlete feels empowered and capable.
- **Negative Self-Talk:** On the other hand, a fixed or negative mindset often leads to destructive self-talk. An athlete might

dwell on their weaknesses, magnify their mistakes, or doubt their abilities. This negative self-talk erodes confidence, making the athlete more likely to feel anxious or unprepared in competitive situations.

4. Handling Pressure and Expectations

- **Mindset Influences Stress Management:** Confidence under pressure is largely a product of mindset. Athletes with a positive, growth-oriented mindset are better equipped to handle stress because they see high-pressure situations as opportunities to showcase their skills and grow. This outlook reduces performance anxiety and boosts confidence, as the athlete is focused on performing well rather than fearing failure.
- **Expectations and Self-Compassion:** A healthy mindset also includes self-compassion—understanding that mistakes are part of the learning process. Athletes who are kind to themselves and maintain realistic expectations are more likely to stay confident, even when things don't go perfectly. This self-compassion prevents the athlete from being overly self-critical, which can diminish confidence.

5. Preparation and Visualization

- **Mindset Drives Effective Preparation:** Confidence is often a by-product of thorough preparation. Athletes with a strong mindset are diligent in their training, knowing that the work they put in will pay off in competition. This preparation reinforces their confidence, as they feel ready and capable when it's time to perform.

- **Visualization as a Confidence Booster:** Athletes who regularly practice visualization—imagining themselves succeeding in their sport—tend to have higher confidence levels. Visualization helps solidify a positive mindset by creating mental images of success, which the brain then associates with actual performance. This mental rehearsal builds confidence by making success feel familiar and achievable.

Mindset is the foundation of confidence. A positive, growth-oriented mindset encourages self-belief, resilience, and constructive self-talk, all of which are essential for maintaining confidence in competitive sports. By cultivating a strong mindset, athletes can develop the confidence needed to face challenges head-on, perform under pressure, and achieve their full potential.

Main takeaway from this Chapter:

- You should embrace visualization as a powerful tool for success by vividly imagining herself performing flawlessly on the volleyball court. This involves creating detailed mental images that engage all your senses, focusing not only on the outcomes but also on the processes leading to success.
- By incorporating emotions and confidence into your visualizations and consistently practicing these techniques, you can align your mind with your physical abilities, making your movements more fluid and your performance more consistent.

- Coupled with physical practice, visualization will help you build confidence, reduce anxiety, and ultimately transform you into the player you aspire to be, exceeding your own expectations and laying a strong foundation for future success.

CHAPTER 4: THE BATTLEFIELD

"I am not the most physical person, not the tallest, not the skinniest. You can't listen to anybody. Just know your dreams. Know how hard you can work. Work hard, have fun doing it, and you can really make it places that you really never thought you would. Dedication, passion and heart gets you where you want to be."

– Lindsey Berg
(former American volleyball setter
who won silver medals at
the 2008 Beijing Olympics)

The Court as a Field for Training and Self-Discovery

During training, imagine that you are a promising volleyball player who has always been known for your natural talent and athleticism. Throughout your early years in the sport, you rarely had to push yourself beyond your comfort zone during practice, yet still managed to perform well in games.

However, as you advanced to a higher level of competition, you noticed that your performance was plateauing. Despite your potential, you were not making the impact on the court that you or your coaches expected. You were often out of position, your reactions were slower, and your spikes lacked the power they once had.

During a particularly tough game, you realized that you were being outplayed by opponents who seemed to be better prepared and more focused. Frustrated and confused, you reflected on your recent practices and recognized a troubling pattern - you hadn't been giving your all during training. You had been going through the motions, treating practice as a routine rather than an opportunity to improve. This complacency was now manifesting in your game performance, and you knew something had to change.

What Should You Do?

Treat Each Practice as If It Were a Championship Final

To overcome this complacency and reach your full potential, you need to approach every training session with the same intensity and focus that you would bring to a championship final. This mindset shift is crucial because **how you train directly influences how you perform in games**. By treating each practice as if it were the most important event of the season, you can ensure that you are constantly pushing yourself to improve, building the habits and resilience needed to excel under pressure.

The Importance of Training with Intensity and Purpose (The "WHY")

1. Set Clear Objectives for Each Training Session

Before each practice, you should take a few moments to set specific, measurable goals for the session. These objectives could be focused on improving a particular skill, such as increasing the accuracy of his-her serves or enhancing his-her footwork on defense. For example, you might set a goal to complete 50 consecutive serves without a mistake or to execute 10 perfect spikes during a drill.

By establishing clear objectives, you will have a concrete target to aim for during practice, which helps maintain focus and motivation. These goals should be challenging but attainable, ensuring that you are always working towards progress without becoming overwhelmed.

You need to know your **WHY**. What is your reason for practice and for what you work hard for?

Danny Uribe explained in the book "*The Volleyball Psychology Workbook: How to Use Advanced Sports Psychology to Succeed on the Volleyball Court*" that after a competitive season that brings a lot of stress on your body, it requires some recovery time. This recovery becomes a problem when skipping workouts becomes a habit. Without a true sense of motivation, it becomes difficult to be committed on a diet or gym sessions. And when you are an aspiring athlete, this makes all the difference. So, you must know the reason you are working hard even between seasons.

2. Fully Engage in Every Drill, Giving 100% Effort

Once practice begins, you must commit to giving your absolute best in every drill, no matter how repetitive or physically demanding it may be. This means not just going through the motions but fully engaging mentally and physically in each activity. Whether you are practicing basic footwork, running sprints, or working on advanced team strategies, you need to approach each drill with the intensity of a game situation.

Even when fatigue sets in or the drills become monotonous, you should remind yourself that every moment of practice is an opportunity to get better. Pushing through discomfort and staying focused when others might slack off is what separates good athletes from great ones. By consistently giving 100% effort, you will develop the stamina, discipline, and mental toughness that are crucial for high-level competition.

3. **Use Self-Talk Techniques to Maintain High Focus and Motivation**

To stay motivated and maintain focus throughout practice, you can use positive self-talk techniques. Self-talk involves consciously directing your inner dialogue to reinforce a strong, positive mindset. For instance, when you feel your energy waning, you can repeat affirmations like:

"I am strong, I am focused, and I am improving."

"Every rep count, every drill matters."

This practice not only keeps his motivation high but also helps to drown out any negative thoughts that might creep in, such as doubts about his abilities or frustrations over mistakes. By controlling his self-talk, you can stay mentally engaged and resilient, even during the toughest parts of practice.

What Will Be the Result?

By consistently applying these principles, you will notice significant improvements in both his training and game performance. When you treat each practice with the intensity and focus of a championship final, your skills will sharpen, your stamina will increase, and your confidence will grow. The habits you build in practice - precision in execution, mental toughness, and relentless effort - will naturally translate to your performance in games.

As a result, your game play will become more consistent and effective. Your reactions on the court will be quicker, your decision-making more instinctive, and your overall performance more impactful.

Teammates and coaches will start to notice the change in your game, recognizing the dedication and effort you bring to every match. Ultimately, by training with purpose and intensity, you will unlock your full potential and establish yourself as a key player on your team.

Examples from Elite Athletes:

A great example of an elite athlete who exemplified this approach is **Kobe Bryant**, one of the most dedicated and successful basketball players in NBA history. Bryant was known for his relentless work ethic and the intensity he brought to every practice. He famously practiced at game speed, treating every drill as if he were in the final minutes of a championship game.

Bryant would arrive at the gym hours before his teammates, often practicing alone, working on every aspect of his game - footwork, shooting, conditioning - until he had perfected it. He would push himself to exhaustion, believing that the effort he put into practice would pay off in games. This mindset not only honed his skills to an elite level but also built the mental toughness that allowed him to perform under pressure and lead his teams to multiple championships.

Kobe's approach to practice is a powerful reminder that the way you train directly impacts the way you perform. By treating every practice as a crucial step toward greatness, athletes like you can build the foundation for consistent excellence in their sport.

Courtnay Dauwalter, an elite ultra-marathon runner, famously winning three of ultra-running's most epic races during the span of about nine weeks in the year of 2023 – Western States 100, Hardrock 100, and Ultra-Trail du Mont-Blanc, talks about her eagerness to enter the "pain cave" when she is racing.

Dauwalter explained about the "pain cave" by citing a cross country skiing coach that she had in high school. He would always remind her to believe in her capacity to push past that moment when it feels like you have nothing left. She said: "Having someone who believed in me so wholeheartedly that I could trust to keep pushing was important because it is hard to do that when you are in any age, but for sure it is hard to do when you are a teenager. It is the idea that you feel like you are about to die and yet you are telling me there is more to push past that. That's hard to learn. I feel really lucky that I had coach and to learn about that mental side of sports and digging deeper than you think."

Main takeaway from this Chapter:

- To unlock your full potential, you must treat each practice as if it were a championship final, approaching every session with the same intensity and focus that he would bring to a high-stakes game.
- This mindset shift is crucial because the way you train directly impacts your game performance. By setting clear, challenging objectives for each session, fully engaging in every drill with maximum effort, and using positive self-talk to maintain focus, you can build the habits and mental toughness necessary for high-level competition.
- Know your reason, your WHY of what you practice for and what you work hard for. Most successful volleyball players who maintain high levels of performance have a desire inside of them to continue pushing themselves.

CHAPTER 5: DISCIPLINE AS A FOUNDATION

"The best thing we can do is take care of the things we have control of and not be concerned with things we can't. We can control our standard of training, preparation and commitment to executing our system at a high level each time we take the floor."
– Alan Knipe
(American volleyball coach
of men's national volleyball team
during the 2012 London Olympics)

The Role of Consistency and Routine in Development

Imagine that you are a talented volleyball player who have always been passionate about the game. You have been playing for a few years now and have shown flashes of talent, particularly in your powerful serves and quick reflexes on defense.

However, as the competition in your league has intensified, you have noticed that some of your teammates and opponents, who seemed less talented initially, are now outshining you on the court. This realization frustrates you because you know you have the natural ability to excel, but your performance has plateaued.

Upon reflection, you realized that your lack of a disciplined routine was holding you back. Your training was irregular, often dependent on how you felt that day, and your diet and sleep patterns were inconsistent. You knew that if you wanted to reach your full potential and perform consistently at a high level, you needed to commit to a disciplined approach to your training and lifestyle.

What Should You Do?

You begin by setting specific, measurable goals for each practice session, focusing on areas where you know you can improve, like your footwork and consistency in setting. You also start arriving at practice early to work on your serves and stays late to do extra conditioning. Outside of practice, you spend time studying the game - watching videos of professional players to learn new techniques.

Establish and Maintain a Disciplined Routine

To overcome your inconsistency and unlock your full potential, you must establish a disciplined routine where every day counts. Discipline is the foundation of long-term success, as it ensures that progress is steady and continuous. By committing to a structured plan and integrating healthy habits into your daily life, you can build the consistency needed to achieve his goals.

You can set a long-term goal (play with the Division 1 on a specific College) along with short term goals (specific) to help you reach your objective. Make sure that the goal is not too easy and not impossibly tough. You need to test your limits but also give you a sense of believe that you can accomplish what you have set out to accomplish.

Andrew Snow explained about how small changes can unlock a new level of fitness over time in the book *"Run Elite: Train and Think Like the*

Greatest Runners of All Time". For example, a permanent diet change, a regular lifting regimen, and consistent quality sleep are all simply decisions that elite athletes make that an amateur athlete do not. Snow goes on to say that an average person pursues what is guaranteed and reasonable; the elite person pursues the big goal that they really want, regardless of what they "should" do.

In our previous example, as the season progresses, your hard work starts to pay off. Your footwork becomes more agile, your sets more accurate, and your overall game more consistent. your coach and teammates notice the difference, praising you for your improvement and newfound dedication. Even when the matches get tough, your commitment and effort give you an edge. You are no longer just a player with potential; you have become one of the most reliable and effective players on the team.

How Discipline Shapes an Athlete's Character?

Below are three actions you can start today to improve your consistency in training and performance that can shape your character:

1. **Create a Weekly Training Plan and Follow It Religiously:** The first step for you is to create a detailed weekly training plan that outlines specific workouts, skills drills, and recovery sessions. This plan should be designed to target all areas of his game, including strength, endurance, technical skills, and mental preparation. For example, your weekly plan might include

weight training on Mondays, technical drills on Tuesdays, endurance runs on Wednesdays, and so on.

Once the plan is in place, you must commit to following it without excuses. This means showing up to train even when you are tired, unmotivated, or facing external pressures. The key to building discipline is consistency - by adhering to his plan every day, you will develop the habit of discipline, making it easier to stay on track over the long term.

2. **Integrate Healthy Habits into Your Daily Life:** Discipline extends beyond the field or gym; it also involves the choices you make in your daily life. To support your training, you need to integrate healthy habits that enhance your physical and mental well-being. This includes maintaining a balanced diet that provides the necessary nutrients for energy and recovery, getting adequate sleep each night to allow your body to rest and repair, and staying hydrated throughout the day.

   Additionally, you should incorporate mental practices such as meditation or mindfulness to reduce stress and improve focus. By establishing these healthy habits, you will create a lifestyle that supports your athletic goals and ensures you are always ready to perform at your best.

3. **Use a Training Journal to Track Your Progress and Adjust as Needed:** To stay disciplined and accountable, you should keep a training journal where you record your daily workouts,

diet, sleep patterns, and overall well-being. This journal will serve as a valuable tool for tracking your progress and identifying patterns in your performance. For example, if you notice that your energy levels dip on certain days, you can look back at your journal to see if your diet or sleep was inadequate.

The journal also allows you to adjust your routine as needed. If a particular workout is not producing the desired results, you can modify it or add new exercises to target specific areas. By regularly reviewing his journal, you will stay in tune with your body's needs and ensure that your training remains effective and aligned with your goals.

What Will Be the Result?

By establishing and maintaining a disciplined routine, you will experience significant improvements in his consistency and performance. Daily discipline will strengthen both his body and mind, making progress inevitable. As you become more consistent in your training, your skills will sharpen, your endurance will increase, and your mental focus will become more resilient.

This disciplined approach will also provide you with a solid foundation to face greater challenges in your sport. Whether it's a tough opponent, a high-pressure match, or the grind of a long season, you will be prepared to handle it because your discipline has ingrained the habits and mindset needed for success. Over time, this consistency will translate into standout performances, earning you the respect of your coaches, teammates, and competitors.

Example from an Elite Athlete

A prime example of an elite athlete who embodies discipline is **Cristiano Ronaldo**, one of the most accomplished and celebrated footballers in the history of the sport. Born in Madeira, Portugal, in 1985, Ronaldo's rise to global stardom began at Sporting CP before moving to Manchester United in 2003. At Manchester United, Ronaldo won three Premier League titles, a UEFA Champions League title, and the Ballon d'Or in 2008, solidifying his place among the world's elite players.

In 2009, Ronaldo transferred to Real Madrid for a then-world record fee, where he further cemented his legacy. During his time at Real Madrid, Ronaldo won four more UEFA Champions League titles, two La Liga titles, and multiple individual accolades, including four additional Ballon d'Or awards (2013, 2014, 2016, 2017). He became the club's all-time leading scorer with over 450 goals.

Ronaldo's success is not only due to his natural talent but also his extraordinary work ethic and dedication to training. He is known for his rigorous training regime, which includes intense physical workouts, technical drills, mental preparation, and a meticulous diet to optimize his performance.

Ronaldo's discipline extends to all aspects of his life. He avoids distractions, prioritizes rest and recovery, and is constantly seeking ways to improve. His training routine is so consistent that he has maintained peak physical condition well into his 30s, an age when many soccer players begin to decline.

Ronaldo's discipline is a key factor in his longevity and success. By committing to a disciplined lifestyle, he has consistently performed at the highest level, winning numerous championships, breaking records, and earning accolades as one of the best athletes in the world. Ronaldo's career is a testament to the power of combining natural talent with relentless effort and discipline, making him one of the greatest athletes of all time.

You, like Ronaldo, can achieve remarkable success by embracing discipline as the foundation of your training and lifestyle. By doing so, you will develop the consistency, resilience, and excellence needed to reach your full potential in volleyball and beyond.

Main takeaway from this Chapter:

- To overcome inconsistency and unlock your full potential, you must establish and maintain a disciplined routine that you follow daily, ensuring steady and continuous progress.
- This involves creating a detailed weekly training plan that targets all aspects of your game, committing to it without excuses, and integrating healthy habits such as a balanced diet,

adequate sleep, and mental practices like meditation into your daily life.

- By keeping a training journal link to site to track your progress and make necessary adjustments, you can stay disciplined and accountable. Over time, this disciplined approach will sharpen your skills, increase your endurance, and build the mental resilience needed to excel, leading to consistent, standout performances on the court and earning the respect of your coaches and teammates.
- Discipline as the foundation of your training and lifestyle will bring you consistency, resilience, and excellence needed to reach your full potential in volleyball and beyond.

CHAPTER 6: SUPPORT AND TEAM

"Volleyball is about recognizing patterns, reacting quickly, and working together to accomplish a shared goal."

\- Karch Kiraly

Indoor, beach volleyball player, head coach of the U.S. women's national volleyball team, leading the team to gold at the 2020 Tokyo Olympic

The Value of Teamwork and the Importance of a Support Network

Imagine that you are a volleyball player who recently joined a new team with high expectations. You were excited to contribute to the team's success, but after a few weeks, you began to feel increasingly isolated.

Despite your efforts on the court, you found it difficult to connect with your teammates, who had already formed close bonds. The lack of connection started affecting your confidence and performance.

Additionally, you sensed that some of your teammates were reluctant to pass you the ball during crucial plays, which only deepened your sense of alienation. The situation escalated when a miscommunication during a critical game led to a lost point and a subsequent argument between you and another teammate.

This conflict created tension within the team, leading to a noticeable drop in their overall performance. You realized that your inability to integrate into the team was not only affecting you personally but was also hurting the team's dynamics and chances of success.

What Should You Do?

Build Healthy and Strong Relationships with Teammates and Coaches

To overcome the feelings of isolation and improve the team's dynamics, you must take proactive steps to build healthy and strong relationships with your teammates and coaches.

A cohesive team, where members trust and support one another, is essential for achieving collective success. By fostering positive relationships, you can help create an environment where everyone feels valued and motivated to work together toward common goals.

How to Build Healthy Relationships with Coaches and Teammates?

1. Actively Participate in Group Activities off the Court to Strengthen Bonds

You should look for opportunities to engage with your teammates outside of practice and games. Participating in group activities such as team dinners, social outings, or team-building exercises can help break down barriers and foster camaraderie. For example, if the team plans a weekend hike or a casual get-together, you should try to attend and engage with your teammates in a relaxed setting.

These off-court interactions are crucial for building trust and rapport. They allow teammates to get to know each other as individuals, not just as players, which can lead to stronger connections and a more supportive team environment. By actively participating in these activities, you can show his teammates that you are committed to being part of the team, both on and off the court.

2. Communicate Openly and Honestly with Your Teammates and Coaches About Expectations and Challenges

Effective communication is key to resolving conflicts and fostering a positive team dynamic. You should initiate conversations with your teammates and coaches to discuss any concerns or misunderstandings.

For instance, if you feel that you are not being involved in plays as much as you should be, you could approach your teammates and ask for their perspective. You might say, "I have noticed that I am not getting the ball as often during games. Is there something I can improve to earn your trust more?"

3. Open to Receiving Feedback

You should be open to receiving feedback and willing to address any issues that might be causing friction. If there is tension between you and a particular teammate, a one-on-one conversation to clear the air and find common ground can be very effective. Open and honest communication helps to build transparency and mutual respect, which are essential for a cohesive team.

4. Offer Support and Encouragement to Others, Creating an Environment of Trust and Collaboration

To foster a positive team culture, you should make a conscious effort to support and encourage your teammates. This could be as simple as offering words of encouragement after a mistake, recognizing a teammate's good play, or stepping up to help someone who's struggling.

By showing that you are invested in your teammates' success, you can build a reputation as a reliable and supportive team member. Creating an environment of trust and collaboration requires everyone to feel valued and respected.

You should strive to be a positive influence, leading by example and contributing to a culture where every team member feels they have each other's backs. When teammates trust one another, they are more likely to communicate effectively, work together seamlessly, and overcome challenges as a united front.

What Will Be the Result?

A united team that works in synergy is stronger than the sum of its parts. Building a cohesive team will lead to better collective performance and overcoming greater challenges together.

By building strong relationships with your teammates and coaches, you will help create a united team that works in synergy. A team that is cohesive and supportive can achieve much more than a group of individuals working in isolation. As the bonds between teammates strengthen, communication on the court will improve, leading to better coordination and execution during games.

The positive team culture that you help to foster will also reduce conflicts and misunderstandings, allowing the team to focus on their collective goals. With everyone working together, the team will be better equipped to face tough opponents, handle pressure, and push through challenging situations.

In the end, the team's overall performance will improve, and you will feel more connected and confident, knowing that you are an integral part of a successful and united team.

Examples from Elite Coaches

One of the most iconic examples of the power of team unity comes from the 2016 U.S.A. Women's Volleyball Team during the Rio Olympics. The team, led by captain **Christa Dietzen**, faced significant challenges, including tough opponents and the pressure of Olympic competition. Throughout the tournament, the team's success was attributed not just to their physical skills but to the strong bonds and communication they had developed.

Coach **Karch Kiraly** stressed the importance of building trust and open communication within the team. The players frequently engaged in team-building exercises and open discussions, where they could express their thoughts and feelings. This helped to create a culture of mutual respect and collaboration, which was crucial in high-pressure moments. When the team faced Brazil in a tense match, their ability to stay united and support each other was key to their victory.

Coach **Kiraly** explained that "we are all going to fall short. We are going to have some bitter losses, very painful defeats and failures. We have to use those to come back even stronger. That's what makes it sweeter, when we can overcome those and figure out a way to win. The great teams can do that, and those are the gold medal winning teams".

Main takeaway from this Chapter:

- The critical importance of building strong, healthy relationships within a team. When an athlete feels isolated or in conflict with teammates, it can negatively impact both personal performance and the team's dynamics.
- However, by actively engaging with teammates off the court, communicating openly, and offering support, you can help foster a positive, collaborative environment. A united team, built on trust and mutual respect, is far more effective and resilient, capable of achieving greater success together than any individual could alone.
- In team sports, unity is strength, and a cohesive team is essential for reaching collective and individual goals.

CHAPTER 7: THE ART OF DEALING WITH FAILURE

"You have to be willing to fail, to improve."
– Al Scates
(one of the most successful American volleyball coaches of the UCLA men's volleyball team for 50 years)

How to View Defeats as Opportunities for Growth

You are a volleyball player who have always been known for your competitive spirit and consistent performance. However, during the final match of a high-stakes tournament, you made a crucial mistake in the last set. With the score tied and the match on the line, you missed a key spike, causing your team to lose the game.

The defeat was devastating, not just because of the loss, but because you felt personally responsible for the outcome. The disappointment was overwhelming, and you couldn't stop replaying the moment in your mind. As the days passed, you found yourself increasingly demotivated, questioning your abilities and wondering if you had what it takes to succeed at a high level. Your confidence was shaken, and you began to fear that this one mistake might define you as a player.

What Should You Do?

Turn Failure into a Tool for Learning and Growth

To overcome the feelings of demotivation and self-doubt, you need to reframe your perspective on failure. Instead of seeing it as a reflection of your abilities, you should view it as an opportunity for growth.

Every athlete, no matter how skilled, experiences setbacks and makes mistakes. What separates the great athletes from the rest is their ability to learn from these experiences and use them to improve. By turning failure into a learning tool, you can regain your confidence, develop resilience, and emerge as a stronger, more capable player.

Al Scates, who led his UCLA team to 19 NCAA Championships, was a pioneer in the sport, known for his innovative strategies and techniques, which have influenced volleyball coaching at all levels. He applied the following techniques to foster growth and improvement from setbacks:

1. Emphasizing Reflection after Losses

Coach **Scates** encouraged his players to analyze their performance after every loss, focusing not only on what went wrong but on what could be improved. By breaking down matches and identifying specific areas for improvement, players could learn from their mistakes and avoid repeating them in the future.

2. Creating a Learning Environment

Coach **Scates** fostered an environment where failure was seen as an opportunity for growth rather than a defeat. He encouraged players to take risks and experiment with new techniques during practice, understanding that mistakes were part of the learning process.

3. Using Video Analysis

He would meticulously go over game footage with his players, pointing out both errors and positive plays. This visual feedback helped players understand their mistakes and learn the correct techniques more effectively.

4. Focusing on Fundamentals

Coach **Scates** believed that many mistakes stemmed from poor fundamentals. When a player or team failed, he often brought them back to basics, reinforcing the core skills that were essential for success. This approach ensured that players had a solid foundation to build on and helped them correct errors that led to failure.

5. Promoting a Growth Mindset

Coach **Scates** instilled in his players the belief that abilities could be developed through dedication and hard work. By promoting a growth mindset, he encouraged his athletes to view challenges and failures as opportunities to improve and evolve, rather than as insurmountable obstacles.

6. Encouraging Resilience

Coach **Scates** taught his players the importance of resilience—bouncing back from a loss with renewed determination. He emphasized that setbacks were temporary and that the real test of an athlete's character was how they responded to adversity.

7. Reinforcing Team Accountability

After a tough loss, Coach **Scates** would gather the team to discuss what went wrong, but also to plan how to improve moving forward. This collective accountability ensured that everyone was on the same page and committed to learning from their mistakes together.

Practical Techniques to Turn Failures into Learning Experiences

1. Review the Game or Situation, Identifying What Went Wrong and What Can Be Improved

The first step for you is to objectively analyze what happened during the match. You should watch a replay of the game if available, or mentally walk through the sequence of events that led to the mistake.

It is important that you approach this analysis without judgment, focusing on the technical and tactical aspects of your performance rather than personalizing the mistake.

For example, you might realize that you misjudged the timing of your approach or that you were out of position when you attempted the spike. You might also identify external factors, such as miscommunication with a teammate or a change in the opponent's strategy, which contributed to the error.

By breaking down the play, you can gain a clearer understanding of what went wrong and why, which is the first step toward improvement.

2. Develop an Improvement Strategy, Focusing on Specific Drills to Correct the Flaws

Once you have identified the areas that need improvement, you should work with your coach to develop a targeted strategy to address these weaknesses.

This might involve specific drills that focus on timing, positioning, or decision-making under pressure. For example, if the issue was timing, you could incorporate drills that simulate game scenarios, allowing you to practice spiking under various conditions until you feel more confident in your ability to execute the play.

The key here is to be systematic and intentional. By focusing on the areas that contributed to the mistake, you can turn a negative experience into a positive learning opportunity. Each drill should be seen as a step toward mastering the skills needed to avoid similar mistakes in the future.

3. Practice Self-Compassion and Avoid Punishing Yourself Excessively; Use the Experience as Motivation to Improve

As you work on improving your skills, it is essential that you practice self-compassion. It is natural to feel frustrated after a mistake, but excessive self-criticism can be detrimental to both mental and physical performance. You should remind yourself that making mistakes is a part of the learning process, and even the best athletes in the world have faced similar setbacks.

Instead of dwelling on the error, you should focus on what you are doing to improve. Positive self-talk can be a powerful tool in this process. You might tell yourself:

"I am learning and getting better every day."

"This mistake does not define me; it is making me stronger."

By shifting your mindset from self-blame to self-improvement, you can use the experience as fuel to work harder and smarter.

What Will Be the Result?

By turning failure into a learning experience, you will build resilience and mental toughness. The next time you face a high-pressure situation, you will be better prepared, having learned from your past mistakes.

This growth mindset will allow you to recover quickly from setbacks, maintaining your confidence and focus even on challenging circumstances.

As you continue to practice and improve, you will begin to see the results of your hard work. Your performance will become more consistent, and you will feel more in control during crucial moments in a match. The fear of making another mistake will diminish, replaced by a sense of empowerment and readiness to face whatever comes your way.

Ultimately, you will emerge from this experience as a stronger, more self-assured athlete. The ability to learn from failure will become one of your greatest strengths, allowing you to continue growing and achieving success in your sport.

Example from an Elite Athlete

An inspiring example of turning failure into growth is that of **Kerri Walsh Jennings**, one of the most successful beach volleyball players in history. Despite her numerous achievements, including three Olympic gold medals, Walsh Jennings has faced her share of setbacks.

In the 2012 London Olympics, during a crucial match, she and her partner Misty May-Treanor were struggling, and Walsh Jennings made several errors that could have cost them the match. However, instead of letting these mistakes defeat her, she used them as a wake-up call to refocus and adjust her strategy.

Walsh Jennings' ability to quickly analyze her mistakes, communicate with her partner, and make the necessary adjustments was key to their victory in that match and ultimately winning the gold medal. Her resilience and growth mindset have been fundamental to her long-lasting success in a highly competitive sport.

Main takeaway from this Chapter:

- The importance of resilience and a growth mindset in the face of failure. Every athlete will experience setbacks, but what defines their future success is how they respond to these challenges.
- By turning failure into a learning opportunity, practicing self-compassion, and developing targeted improvement strategies, you can transform mistakes into valuable lessons that strengthen your skills and mental fortitude.
- The ability to learn from failure not only makes you more resilient but also prepares you to handle future challenges with greater confidence and poise.

CHAPTER 8: THE BATTLE AGAINST PRESSURE

"I've missed more than 9,000 shots in my career.
I've lost almost 300 games. Twenty-six times,
I've been trusted to take the game-winning shot and missed.
I've failed over and over and over again in my life.
And that is why I succeed."
— Michael Jordan

Strategies for Dealing with Internal and External Pressure

Imagine that you are a key player on your college volleyball team, known for your powerful spikes and strategic plays. Your team have made it to the championship finals, and the stakes could not be higher.

The match is tied, and they are heading into the final set. As the pressure mounts, you begin to feel the weight of the expectations placed on you.

You are acutely aware that your performance could determine the outcome of the match. The crowd is loud, your heart is racing, and you can feel the tension in every muscle. Doubts start to creep in—what if you miss a critical spike? What if you make a mistake that costs your team the championship?

The pressure is intense, and you find yourself questioning whether you can deliver in this decisive moment. You have faced high-pressure situations before, but this feels different. The fear of failure is threatening to paralyze you, and you know that if you do not find a way to manage the pressure, it could impact your performance and the team's chances of victory.

What Should You Do?

Use Pressure as an Opportunity to Show Your Best

In moments like this, you need to reframe your mindset around pressure. Instead of seeing it as a burden, you should view it as an opportunity to showcase your skills and rise to the occasion.

Pressure does not have to be something that paralyzes; it can be the catalyst that brings out an athlete's best performance. By embracing the pressure and using it to fuel her focus and determination, you can turn this high-stakes moment into an opportunity to excel.

How to Maintain Calm and Focus in Decisive Moments

1. Practice Breathing Techniques to Control Nervousness during High-Pressure Moments

The first step for you is to regain control of your physiological responses to pressure. When anxiety hits, the body's natural response is to increase heart rate and breathing, which can escalate feelings of panic. To counteract this, you should practice deep breathing techniques designed to calm the nervous system and refocus the mind.

A simple technique is diaphragmatic breathing, where you inhale deeply through your nose, allowing your abdomen to expand, hold the breath for a moment, and then exhale slowly through your mouth.

This type of breathing helps to slow the heart rate, reduce tension, and bring a sense of calm. By focusing on your breath, you can anchor yourself in the present moment, preventing your mind from spiralling into worry about what might go wrong.

2. Simulate High-Pressure Situations during Training

To prepare for the pressure of critical moments in a game, you should incorporate high-pressure simulations into your training. This involves creating practice scenarios that mimic the intensity and stakes of a championship final. For example, during practice, your coach might set up drills where the team must score a point under strict time constraints, or where you are required to make a crucial spike with all eyes on you.

These simulations help desensitize you to pressure, teaching your body and mind how to stay calm and focused even when the stakes are high. By repeatedly practicing under these conditions, you will become more accustomed to handling pressure, making it less likely to overwhelm you during actual games.

3. Focus on the Present, Concentrating on Each Individual Action Instead of the Final Result

One of the most effective ways for you to manage pressure is to focus on the present moment, rather than getting caught up in the potential outcome of the game.

Instead of thinking about the championship title or what might happen if you fail, you should concentrate on each individual action you need to take - whether it is positioning yourself correctly, executing a precise spike, or communicating effectively with your teammates.

By breaking down the game into smaller, manageable tasks, you can maintain your focus and composure. This mindfulness approach allows you to stay in the moment, where you have control, rather than letting your mind wander to future uncertainties.

This shift in focus not only reduces anxiety but also enhances performance, as your energy is directed toward the actions that matter most in the moment.

What Will Be the Result?

By applying these strategies, you will learn to thrive under pressure rather than being paralyzed by it. You will be able to harness the energy that comes with high-stakes moments and channel it into focused, deliberate action. Instead of fearing the pressure, you will come to see it as an opportunity to demonstrate her abilities and lead your team to success.

Over time, this ability to perform under pressure will become one of your greatest strengths. You will gain a reputation as a clutch player - someone who can be relied upon to deliver in the most critical moments.

This mental toughness will not only enhance your performance in volleyball but will also serve you well in other areas of life where pressure is inevitable.

Example from an Elite Athlete

A well-known example of an athlete thriving under pressure is **Kerri Walsh Jennings** during the 2004 Athens Olympics. Walsh Jennings, along with her partner Misty May-Treanor, faced immense pressure in the gold medal beach volleyball match against Brazil. Despite the high stakes and the pressure of representing their country (U.S.A.) on the world's biggest stage, Walsh Jennings remained calm and focused, using her nerves to fuel her performance.

She employed deep breathing techniques to stay centered and maintained her focus on each play, rather than the overall outcome. This approach allowed her to perform at her peak, leading her team to a decisive victory and securing the gold medal. Walsh Jennings' ability to thrive under pressure became a defining characteristic of her career, contributing to her status as one of the greatest beach volleyball players of all time.

Main takeaway from this Chapter:

- High-stakes moments are an inevitable part of competitive sports, and how an athlete responds to these moments can determine their success.
- By using pressure as an opportunity to show their best, practicing techniques to stay calm, simulating pressure in training, and focusing on the present moment, athletes can turn potential anxiety into a powerful tool for performance.
- The ability to manage pressure not only enhances individual performance but also contributes to the overall success of the team. Pressure is not something to be feared, but rather embraced as a catalyst for enhancement.

CHAPTER 9: OVERCOMING LIMITS

"Limits, like fears,
are often just an illusion."
- Michael Jordan

Imagine you are a volleyball player, known for your aggressive style of play. Whether it is going for a tough serve, attempting a block against a stronger opponent, or trying to spike the ball in a tight spot, you thrive on taking risks. You have always been drawn to the thrill of pushing your limits, constantly challenging yourself to reach new heights on the court.

We can list five benefits of taking risks:

1. Improved Skill Development

By consistently challenging yourself, you force your body and mind to adapt to more difficult situations. For example, attempting tougher serves or more complex plays helps you refine your techniques and discover new strategies. Each time you take a calculated risk, whether successful or not, you learn something valuable that contributes to your overall skill set.

2. Increased Confidence

As you push yourself out of your comfort zone and succeed in difficult scenarios, your confidence naturally grows. The more risks you take and the more often they pay off, the more you start to believe in your abilities. This self-confidence becomes a critical asset during high-pressure moments in games, where believing in yourself can make the difference between winning and losing.

3. Enhanced Mental Toughness

Taking risks often means facing failure or setbacks. However, by embracing these challenges, you develop mental resilience. Learning to bounce back from a missed spike or a failed block strengthens your ability to stay focused and determined, even when things don't go as planned. This mental toughness is crucial in competitive sports, where the ability to recover quickly from mistakes can define your success.

4. Leadership and Inspiration

Your willingness to take risks and challenge yourself sets a powerful example for your teammates. They see your courage and determination, and it inspires them to push their own limits. As a result, you often emerge as a leader on the team, not just because of your skills but because of your attitude and the energy you bring to every game and practice.

5. Greater Opportunities for Success

In volleyball, as in life, the biggest rewards often come from the biggest risks. By taking chances - whether it is going for a difficult shot or stepping up in crucial moments - you create more opportunities to make game-changing plays.

While playing it safe may keep you from making mistakes, it is the risks that often lead to the most spectacular successes, the ones that can turn the tide of a match or even define a season.

Challenge Yourself to Step out of your Comfort Zone and Surpass Self-Imposed Limits

To overcome any plateau, you need to recognize that the same routines and methods that got you to your current level may not be enough to push you further.

Progress often stalls when an athlete becomes too comfortable with their current training regimen. To break through this stagnation, you must be willing to challenge yourself, step out of your comfort zone, and push beyond the limits you may have unconsciously set for yourself.

This requires setting more ambitious goals, experimenting with new techniques, and adopting a mindset focused on growth and adaptability.

How to Step out of your Comfort Zone?

1. Set More Ambitious Goals and Break Them Down into Achievable Steps

The first step for you is to reassess your goals. While your current objectives may have been sufficient in the past, they might no longer be challenging enough to drive continued improvement.

You should set more ambitious, long-term goals that push the boundaries of what you believe is possible for yourself. For example, instead of merely maintaining your current spike accuracy, you could aim to increase your spike speed by 20% within the next six months.

Once these ambitious goals are set, you should break them down into smaller, actionable steps. These steps should be specific and time-bound, providing a clear roadmap for how to achieve the larger objective.

For instance, the first step might involve increasing your upper body strength through targeted weight training, followed by incorporating speed-focused drills into your practice routine. By breaking down the goals, you can focus on incremental progress, which is both motivating and manageable.

2. Introduce New Techniques and Training Methods That Challenge Different Aspects of Your Skills

To push past your plateau, you need to introduce variety and challenge into your training.

This might involve experimenting with new techniques, incorporating different training methods, or working on areas of your game that you have previously overlooked. For example, if you have primarily focused on power in your spikes, you could start working on increasing his precision or developing a wider range of shots.

Additionally, you could benefit from cross-training or participating in other sports that challenge different muscle groups and skills. For instance, adding agility drills or even practicing martial arts could improve your footwork and reaction time on the volleyball court.

By challenging your body and mind in new ways, you can break through the monotony of your routine and stimulate new growth.

3. Keep a Progress Journal, Documenting Each Small Victory as Evidence of Your Growth

As you embark on this journey to break through your plateau, it is essential that you track your progress. A progress journal link can be an invaluable tool for this purpose. In your journal, you should document each training session, noting any improvements, challenges, and insights.

Recording these details helps you stay focused on your goals and provides a tangible record of your efforts.

More importantly, the journal allows you to celebrate small victories along the way. Whether it is a slight increase in spike speed or improved agility during a drill, these achievements are evidence of your growth and serve as motivation to keep pushing forward. Over time, this documentation will show you that, despite the plateau, you are still progressing, which will reinforce your commitment to breaking through to the next level.

What Will Be the Result?

By challenging yourself to step out of your comfort zone and break through self-imposed limits, you will experience renewed progress in your performance.

As you pursue more ambitious goals and experiments with new training methods, you will unlock new levels of physical and mental development. This process will not only improve your skills on the court but also strengthen your mindset, making you more resilient and adaptable in the face of future challenges.

You will find that your plateau was not the peak of your abilities but rather a temporary hurdle that, once overcome, leads to even greater heights. As you continue to push your boundaries, you will discover new dimensions of your potential, which will reinvigorate your passion for the sport and solidify your place as a top-performing athlete.

Example from an Elite Athlete

A great example of an athlete who broke through a plateau is **Serena Williams**, one of the greatest tennis players of all time. After achieving numerous milestones early in her career, Serena faced periods where her progress seemed to stall, and her performance plateaued.

Rather than accepting this as a limitation, Serena continually challenged herself by setting new goals, adopting innovative training methods, and pushing her body and mind beyond what she had previously believed possible.

Serena incorporated various training techniques, including strength and conditioning programs that targeted specific areas of her game. She also embraced mental conditioning, working with psychologists to develop greater mental resilience and focus.

By continually pushing her limits and refusing to settle, Serena not only broke through her plateaus but also returned to the top of the tennis world multiple times, even after setbacks like injuries and breaks from the sport.

By embracing risk and constantly challenging yourself, you unlock your full potential as an athlete. You become more skilled, confident, and mentally strong, all of which contribute to your success on the court.

Moreover, your fearless approach not only elevates your own game but also inspires those around you, making you a pivotal player on any team. Taking risks in volleyball is not about being reckless – it is about believing in your ability to rise to the occasion and reach new heights.

Main takeaway from this Chapter:

- Hitting a plateau in performance is not the end but an opportunity for growth. When progress stalls, it is a signal that the current methods and goals may need to be revaluated and adjusted.
- By setting more ambitious goals, experimenting with new techniques, and tracking progress diligently, you can break through your plateaus and reach new levels of performance.
- True growth happens when you challenge yourself to move beyond comfort and embrace the discomfort of pushing your limits. In doing so, you unlock new potential, both physically and mentally, and continue to progress toward greatness.

CHAPTER 10: THE SPIRIT OF COMPETITION

"Don't fire your opponents up.
If they are down, don't' tick them off.
Let them stay down."
– Sinjin Smith
(Pioneer of Professional Beach Volleyball,
his efforts and success helped pave the way
for the sport's inclusion in the
1996 Atlanta Olympics)

Cultivating Healthy Competitiveness

You are a volleyball player with a strong desire to excel in your sport. As you compete in various tournaments, you find yourself increasingly focused on how you measure up against other players.

You constantly compare your skills, achievements, and even your physical attributes to those of your teammates and opponents. If another player outperforms you in a game, you feel inadequate and begin to question your abilities.

This habit of comparison has begun to erode your confidence and enjoyment of the game. Instead of focusing on your own growth, you become consumed with the idea of outshining others, which only adds pressure and anxiety to your performance.

As a result, your game suffers. You are distracted, your self-esteem fluctuates based on how others are performing, and you find it difficult to stay motivated. The joy of playing volleyball, which once fueled your passion, is now overshadowed by your obsession with being the best in comparison to others.

What Should you Do?

Adopt a Healthy Competition Mindset, Focusing on Being the Best Version of Yourself

To break free from the negative cycle of comparison, you need to shift your mindset towards healthy competition. Rather than seeing other players as benchmarks for yours her success, you should focus on your own personal growth and development.

Healthy competition is about pushing oneself to achieve personal excellence, not about outperforming others to validate one's worth. By redefining success as progress in your own journey, you can reclaim your confidence and find renewed motivation in your sport.

How Desire to Win Drives Excellence?

1. Redefine Success as Personal Progress, Rather than Merely Beating Others

The first step is to redefine what success means to you. Instead of measuring your worth by whether you win or lose against others, you should set personal goals that are based on your own improvement. For example, you might focus on increasing the consistency of your serves, improving your defensive skills, or mastering a new technique. Success, in this context, is about achieving these personal milestones rather than merely outperforming your teammates or opponents.

By setting and pursuing goals that are independent of others' performance, you can track your own progress and find satisfaction in your achievements. This approach helps you maintain a positive and constructive mindset, even if others are performing well or if you face setbacks in competition.

2. Use Competition as a Motivator to Push Yourself Harder, but Without Letting It Dictate Your Worth

Competition can be a powerful motivator when approached with the right mindset. You should use the presence of strong competitors as inspiration to push yourself harder, but you must be careful not to let your self-worth be determined by how you compare to others. Instead, you can view each match as an opportunity to test your own limits and see how much you have grown.

For example, if you play against a particularly skilled opponent, you can see it as a chance to learn and improve. You might challenge yourself to stay focused, execute your strategies more effectively, or maintain your composure under pressure.

By seeing competition as a tool for self-improvement rather than a measure of worth, you can maintain a healthy perspective and continue to grow as an athlete.

3. Practice Gratitude and Acknowledge Others' Achievements as a Way to Learn and Grow

You should practice gratitude for your own abilities and achievements, while also acknowledging and respecting the successes of others. This does not mean downplaying your own goals, but rather appreciating the skills and efforts of your competitors as opportunities to learn. For example, if a teammate excels in a particular aspect of the game, you can observe their techniques, ask for tips, and use their success as a learning experience.

Practicing gratitude also involves celebrating your own progress, no matter how small. By focusing on your own journey and being grateful for the opportunities to compete and improve, you can foster a more positive and supportive mindset. This approach not only reduces the stress of constant comparison but also builds a stronger, more resilient mental foundation.

What Will Be the Result?

By adopting a healthy competition mindset, you will develop unshakable confidence in your abilities. You will become a more balanced competitor, able to use competition as a tool for continuous evolution without being weighed down by comparisons.

As you focus on your own progress and appreciate the achievements of others, you will experience a renewed sense of motivation and enjoyment in your sport.

Your performance will improve as you learn to stay present and focused on your own game, rather than being distracted by what others are doing.

This mindset will also make you more resilient in the face of challenges, as you will be driven by your own goals and growth rather than external validation. Ultimately, you will find that true success lies not in surpassing others, but in becoming the best version of herself.

Example from an Elite Athlete

A notable example of an athlete who mastered the art of healthy competition is **Simone Biles**, one of the greatest gymnasts of all time. Throughout her career, Biles has faced intense competition, both from within her team and from international rivals.

However, Biles has consistently emphasized the importance of focusing on her own performance rather than comparing herself to others. She sets her own goals and measures her success by her personal progress and achievements, rather than by how she stacks up against her competitors.

Biles uses competition as a motivator to push herself to new heights, but she remains grounded in her own journey. She acknowledges the talents of her peers and learns from them, but she never lets comparison undermine her confidence.

This mindset has allowed her to achieve unprecedented success in gymnastics, including multiple Olympic gold medals and world championships, while maintaining a positive and healthy relationship with her sport.

Main takeaway from this Chapter:

- The importance of adopting a healthy competition mindset. Constantly comparing oneself to others can erode confidence and distract from personal growth.
- You should focus on being the best version of yourself, using competition as a motivator for self-improvement rather than a measure of self-worth.
- By redefining success as personal progress, practicing gratitude, and acknowledging the achievements of others, athletes can build resilience, confidence, and a more balanced approach to competition.

CHAPTER 11: VICTORY AS A REFLECTION OF EFFORT

"Success is no accident. It is hard work, perseverance, learning, studying, sacrifice and most of all, love of what you are doing or learning to do."
- Pelé
(Soccer player)

Pelé is widely regarded as one of the greatest footballers of all time. Born Edson Arantes do Nascimento in 1940, Pelé's achievements on the football field are legendary, and his impact on the sport is unparalleled.

Pelé is the only player in history to have won three FIFA World Cups (1958, 1962, 1970). His first victory came at the age of 17, making him the youngest player to win a World Cup. His performances in these tournaments helped solidify Brazil's dominance in world football.

Pelé's style of play, characterized by his incredible skill, vision, and flair, has inspired generations of footballers. He is often referred to as "The King of Football" and remains a symbol of excellence in the sport. His philosophy on achieving greatness, emphasizes the importance of dedication, passion, and hard work in reaching one's goals.

Understand That True Victory is the Result of Consistent and Dedicated Effort over Time

To overcome any frustration, you need to shift your perspective on what success really means. It is easy to become discouraged when comparing oneself to others, but it is important to remember that everyone's journey is different.

True victory is not about achieving immediate results or outperforming others; it is about staying committed to the process of improvement, day in and day out. You must understand that success is a marathon, not a sprint, and that consistent, dedicated effort over time is what ultimately leads to lasting achievements.

The Gratification of Achieving Goals through Effort

How Should You Do It?

1. Keep a Detailed Record of your Training, including Hours Dedicated, Techniques Worked on, and Perceived Progress

As we previous mentioned, one of the most effective ways for you to stay motivated and see the value of your hard work is to keep a detailed training journal.

In this journal, you should record every aspect of your training - how many hours you practice, what specific techniques you focus on, any feedback you receive, and how you feel about your progress each day. By keeping this detailed record, you can track your growth over time and recognize patterns in your training.

This documentation will help you see that, even if you are not achieving big milestones yet, you are steadily improving in various aspects of your game. Over time, this record becomes a powerful tool for measuring progress, providing evidence that your dedication is making a difference.

2. Celebrate Small Victories, Recognizing that each Step Forward is Part of the Journey to Success

It is important for you to celebrate the small victories along the way. These might include perfecting a new technique, improving your serve accuracy, or even just feeling more confident on the court. Each of these small achievements is a step forward and should be acknowledged as part of the overall journey to success.

By celebrating these small wins, you can maintain a positive outlook and stay motivated. Recognizing that every bit of progress, no matter how minor it may seem, contributes to your long-term goals helps you stay focused on your personal growth rather than comparing yourself to others.

3. Practice Patience and Persistence, Focusing on the Long Term rather Than Immediate Results

You need to develop patience and persistence, understanding that true success takes time. You should remind yourself that the athletes you admire likely faced their own struggles and setbacks before reaching their current level of success. The key is to stay persistent, continuing to put in the effort and trusting that the results will come in due time.

It is not easy but you should focus on the long-term vision of your career rather than getting discouraged by short-term setbacks or slower progress. By committing to consistent effort and maintaining a positive mindset, you will build the resilience needed to overcome challenges and continue improving over time.

What Will Be the Result?

With continued dedication, you will see victories happen naturally, both on and off the court. As you persist in your training, celebrating small wins and focusing on the long-term goal, you will notice gradual but meaningful improvements in your performance.

Over time, these improvements will accumulate, leading to significant achievements that reflect the hard work and dedication you have invested.

You will also find that this approach benefits other areas of your life. The discipline, patience, and persistence you develop through volleyball will translate into greater resilience and success in academics, relationships, and future career pursuits.

You will come to understand that success is not about quick wins or instant gratification, but about the steady, consistent effort that builds a strong foundation for lasting achievement.

Examples from Elite Athletes

As we have mentioned, **Michael Jordan**'s success did not come overnight. He dedicated countless hours to practice, honing his skills and building the mental toughness that would later define his career.

His relentless work ethic and focus on long-term growth paid off, leading to six NBA championships and numerous accolades. Jordan's story is a testament to the power of consistent effort and dedication over time, proving that true victory is the result of perseverance.

At just 19 years old, **Simone Biles** stepped onto the world's biggest stage at the 2016 Rio Olympics, already hailed as a gymnastics prodigy. But behind the dazzling flips and seemingly effortless routines was a young athlete who had spent countless hours in the gym, honing her skills with relentless dedication.

Day after day, year after year, Biles trained for hours on end, pushing through physical and mental barriers, perfecting every move with a level of precision that few could achieve.

Her hard work culminated in an awe-inspiring performance that earned her Olympic medals, solidifying her as one of the greatest gymnasts of all time.

Bile's story is a powerful testament to the fact that hard work pays off - her success was not a product of luck, but the result of an unwavering commitment to her craft and a willingness to outwork everyone else to achieve her dreams.

Main takeaway from this Chapter:

- True success comes from consistent and dedicated effort over time, not from immediate results or comparisons to others. It's important to keep a detailed record of your progress, celebrate small victories, and maintain patience and persistence as you work toward your goals.
- By focusing on your own journey and committing to steady improvement, you will ultimately achieve the success you seek, both in sports and in life. Success is not an event but a process, and that every step forward, no matter how small, is a meaningful part of that process.
- Success is about the steady, consistent effort that builds a strong foundation for lasting achievement.

CHAPTER 12: TAKE RISKS
DON'T BE AN AVERAGE PLAYER

"A legacy is not about trophies and medals. It's about the lives you touch and the impact you make on the world."
- Kobe Bryant

Imagine you have become more comfortable with your performance on the volleyball court. You had established yourself as a reliable player, known for your consistency and solid technique.

However, despite your progress, you felt that something was still missing. Deep down, you knew that if you wanted to truly stand out and achieve greatness, you could not just play it safe. It was time to take risks.

Understanding the Importance of Taking Risks

After a particularly challenging practice, your Coach gathered the team in a huddle and said:

"Girls, I've seen you all grow tremendously as players, but today I want to talk about something that separates good players from great ones. It's something many are afraid to do, but those who embrace it often find themselves on a path to greatness. I'm talking about taking risks."

You listened closely, intrigued. You had always been cautious on the court, preferring to stick to what you knew worked. But as you looked around at your teammates, you realized that they were all playing it safe, just like you. And if they all continued to do so, they would blend in rather than stand out.

"Think about the greatest athletes in any sport", your Coach continued. "One excellent example is **Caitlin Clark**, a rising star in women's basketball. She doesn't settle for being an ordinary player. Caitlin is bold; she attempts shots that others wouldn't even consider, makes creative passes, and elevates her team's performance to a higher level. She isn't afraid to take risks, and because of that, she's standing out and elevating the game, as well as the reputation of the WNBA."

The Story of Caitlin Clark: Standing Out by Taking Risks

Caitlin Clark, despite her young age, has quickly become one of the most exciting players to watch in women's basketball. Known for her incredible long-range shooting and creative plays, Caitlin did not achieve this level of recognition by playing it safe.

She has a reputation for attempting shots that others would not even consider, making her a standout on the court. But what makes Caitlin truly exceptional is not just her willingness to take risks, but her humility and perspective on success.

In one of her interviews, Caitlin said:

"A record is a record. I don't want it to be the reason people remember me. I hope people remember me for the way I played with a smile on my face, my competitive fire. They can remember the wins but also the fun me and my teammates had together".

This quote highlights her belief that true greatness is not just about personal accolades, but about the joy and passion one brings to the game.

Caitlin also shared that she is always focused on the opinions of those within her team, stating:

"What I really care about is the people inside our locker room, the people that I love to death, the people that have had my back every single second of my career".

This humility and dedication to her teammates are what make her a leader both on and off the court.

Developing the Courage to Take Risks

"But taking risks is not easy," your Coach acknowledged.

"It requires courage, confidence, and a willingness to fail. It means stepping into the unknown, not knowing whether you will succeed or fail, but doing it anyway because that is where growth happens. The greatest players are not afraid of failure – they are afraid of being average", she explained.

You began to understand that taking risks was not about being reckless; it was about having the confidence to try new things, even if it meant making mistakes. You started to see the volleyball court differently - not just as a place to execute what you had practiced, but as a space for creativity and innovation.

"Start small," your Coach advised. "Maybe it is trying a new serve technique, going for a difficult spike, or attempting a dig that seems out of reach. These are the moments where you can start to distinguish yourself as a player. Yes, you might fail a few times, but each time you take that risk, you learn something new. And eventually, you will find yourself making plays that other players would not even attempt."

Embracing the Mindset of a Risk-Taker

You decided to put this new mindset into practice. In the following games and practices, you began pushing yourself to try new things. Instead of sticking to your usual safe serves, you experimented with more aggressive ones.

You started taking more chances on defense, diving for balls that seemed just out of reach, and going for spikes even when the angle was difficult.

At first, there were mistakes. There were moments of frustration when your risks did not pay off. But slowly, you began to see the benefits.

Your serves started to land with more power and precision. Your defensive plays became sharper. Your confidence grew with each successful risk she took, and so did your reputation on the team.

You realized that by stepping out of your comfort zone, you were not just improving your skills – you were becoming a more dynamic, unpredictable player.

Opponents could not easily anticipate your moves because you were always trying something new. And even when you failed, you knew that you were pushing yourself further than most players were willing to go.

Rising Above the Average

The Coach noticed your transformation and could not have been prouder. "This is what I've been talking about," the Coach said after a particularly daring play that had secured the team a crucial point:

"You are not just playing the game—you are redefining it. That is what it takes to rise above the average."

You smiled, feeling a deep sense of satisfaction. You knew you still had a lot to learn and many more risks to take, but you were no longer afraid of the unknown.

You had learned that greatness was not about always succeeding—it was about daring to be different, to challenge the status quo, and to take risks that others would not.

Encouraging Others to Take Risks

As you continued to grow in your new mindset, you also encouraged your teammates to do the same. You reminded them that being average was not enough if they wanted to reach the highest levels of the sport.

You shared the story of Caitlin Clark and other athletes who risked everything to achieve greatness, emphasizing the importance of stepping out of their comfort zones.

Together, the team started to embrace this new philosophy. Practices became more experimental, games more exciting. Each player brought her own unique flair to the court, and the team's performance improved as a result.

Main takeaway from this Chapter:

- Caitlin Clark did not achieve this level of recognition by playing it safe. She has a reputation for attempting shots that others wouldn't even consider, making her a standout on the court. But what makes Caitlin truly exceptional is not just her willingness to take risks, but her humility and perspective on success.
- When you step out of your comfort zone, you are not just improving your skills – you are becoming a more dynamic, unpredictable player.
- When you encourage your team players to embrace the same philosophy, practices became more experimental, games more exciting, and the team's performance improved as a result.

CONCLUSION

As we conclude **"The Art of the Game",** it's important to reflect on the journey you have taken through the chapters of this book. Each chapter has been crafted to guide you not just in becoming a better athlete, but in mastering the mental and emotional aspects of the game that are just as crucial as physical competence.

The lessons you have learned here are not just for your time on the court but are tools for life. The principles of self-awareness, discipline, and resilience will serve you well in all your endeavors, both in sports and beyond.

You began to understand that taking risks is not about being reckless; it is about having the confidence to try new things, even if it meant making mistakes. The volleyball court is not just as a place to execute what you had practiced, but as a space for creativity and innovation.

Remember what Muhammad Ali said: "Champions aren't made in gyms. Champions are made from something they have deep inside them - a desire, a dream, a vision." Have your vision and go for it!

ABOUT THE AUTHORS

As parents of a teenage daughter who is deeply passionate about volleyball, we understand how challenging it can be to find reliable information and build a support network for young athletes. That's why we created Spike Parents - to help our daughter and countless other young athletes and their parents navigate the wonderful yet often turbulent world of youth sports.

We do not claim to be experts, nor do we hold all the answers. We, the parents, were athletes in our youth - though in a different sport, Karate. Both of us hold a 4th degree Black Belt in Karate, and we competed intensely, earning titles at municipal, provincial, national, and Pan-American levels. Additionally, we owned an official CrossFit gym in Brazil, and created an obstacle race called Dark Race. Sports have always been a central part of our lives.

It is not easy to balance youth, sports, school, family, love, friendships, changes in the body, mood swings, and evolving dreams - all at the same time!

Our primary goal is to create and nurture a community of parents and athletes who can play this game together, full of spikes, blocks, defenses, tips, and dives. Hope you enjoyed this guide!

ADDITIONAL RESOURCES

To further enhance your journey as an athlete and continue building on the principles outlined in **"The Art of the Game",** here are some additional resources that can support your growth:

1. Books:

- *"The Volleyball Psychology Workbook: How to Use Advanced Sports Psychology to Succeed on the Volleyball Court"* by Danny Uribe.

  This book explores dynamic exercises and how it can impact your motivation in sports and life. It provides valuable insights into the power of believing that your abilities can be developed through effort and learning.

- *"Run Elite: Train and Think Like the Greatest Runners of All Time"* by Andrew Snow.

  This book explores the concept of mindset and how it can impact your performance in running. It provides valuable insights into the power of believing that excellence in running is not about a genetic gift, it is about consistently doing the things that will yield an outstanding result.

- *"Mindset: The New Psychology of Success"* by Carol S. Dweck.

  This book explores the concept of a growth mindset and how it can impact your success in sports and life. It provides valuable insights into the power of believing that your abilities can be developed through effort and learning.

- *"Relentless: From Good to Great to Unstoppable"* by Tim S. Grover.

Written by the legendary trainer of Michael Jordan, Kobe Bryant, and other elite athletes, this book delves into the mindset required to achieve greatness and maintain a competitive edge.

- *"The Champion's Mind: How Great Athletes Think, Train, and Thrive"* by Jim Afremow.

The book offers practical advice on mental training, motivation, and overcoming challenges, with insights from top athletes across various sports.

2. Documentaries and Films:

- *"The Last Dance"* (Netflix): A documentary series that chronicles Michael Jordan's career and the Chicago Bulls' 1997-98 season, offering a deep dive into the mindset of a champion.

- *"Race"* (Prime Video): This movie follows runner Jesse Owen's journey to win Olympic medals in Germany and become the fastest man alive, showcasing coaching lessons from Larry Snyder.

- *"King Richard"* (Prime Video, Apple): A compelling look at Venus and Serena Williams' journey with their father until they became professional athletes, providing insights into the adversities faced by athletes who dream to play in the professional level.

- "*The Boys in the Boat*" (Prime Video): An inspirational true story of a group of underdogs as they are thrust into spotlight and take on elite rivals from around the world in the Summer Olympics in Berlin. It shows the intersection between rowing skills, physique, and timing to win, providing insights into the pressures faced by athletes at elite level.

4. **Journaling Tools:**

- "*The Volleyball Stat Tracker Player Log Book*" (By Spike Parents): A guided journal that encourages daily reflection on tracking detailed stats, goals, and progress, helping you monitor and celebrate the progress in your volleyball journey, capturing the highlights and milestones of every game.

Made in the USA
Middletown, DE
16 November 2024